KU-430-748

5-MINUTE FINANCE

A Business Owners' Guide to Knowing and Understanding Your Numbers

Christine Nicholson ACMA

Text Copyright © Christine Nicholson 2017

Christine Nicholson has asserted her right in accordance with the
Copyright Designs and Patents Act 1988 to be identified as the
author of this work.

All rights reserved

No part of this publication may be lent, resold, hired out or reproduced
in any form or by any means without prior written permission from the
author and publisher. All rights reserved.
Copyright © 3P Publishing

First published in 2017 in the UK

3P Publishing
C E C, London Road
Corby
NN17 5EU

A catalogue number for this book is available from the British Library

ISBN 978-1-911559-38-2

Dedications:

To my Mum, Avril, for never telling me what I couldn't do;

To Jacinta, Damian, Nigel and Frahana - for getting me to step up to the plate and take a swing!

To all the people who helped me along the way, there are too many to mention – they know who they are.

5-Minute Finance

Table of Contents

INTRODUCTION

"**ACCOUNTING** – is possibly the most boring subject in the world. And it is also one of the most confusing.
But if you want to be rich, long-term, it could be the most important...."

WARNING: This is NOT an accounting book!

WHY I AM WRITING THIS BOOK

I've been working with entrepreneurs and business owners for many years and one of the most common themes is either the fear of numbers in general or lack of understanding of the numbers in their business.

Most commonly it's both.

Many people think that numbers are difficult, like a foreign language. Accountants and Accounting Practices can often charge very high fees for their services – and they get away with it because the mechanics of accounting is poorly understood by business owners.

Many business owners believe that having more advice and support from their accountant increases costs but offers no added value to their businesses, especially larger corporate practices that need to cover higher overheads from a large workforce with high salaries and posh offices.

The clear majority of small business accountants are, at best, passively billing fees for doing the bare minimum of statutory services (tax returns and statutory accounts).

"Finance is very simple, but it's made to look complicated to justify the fees."
www.fool.com

Accounting is a bit like law and IT. There is a "language" used, an unusual and often unnecessary vocabulary to describe the financial activities of the business.

Most accountants are not very entrepreneur friendly.

This can be off-putting for non-finance people.

But not all accountants are the same, and there is a new breed of accounting practice emerging that puts the businesses they support at the heart of the services they offer. They are much more commercially focused than the traditional tax-orientated accountants of the past.

Driven by advances in technology, proactive accountants are providing regular financial reports, growth advice and working in collaboration with the business, as well as the annual accounting and tax services.

This book aims to take the foreign language and turn it into a layman's view of the most basic aspects of finance and how your business numbers work so you can understand them more easily and be more confident about your business finances.

"An investment in knowledge always pays the best interest."
Benjamin Franklin

3

WHO IS THIS BOOK FOR?

If you're reading this book, then you may have been attracted by the title, possibly intrigued by the "five minutes" claim to understand elements of finance in your business.

Principally this book is for those with no time and who don't understand finance!

If you are a business owner and you have less than a full understanding of your accounts, or you think you know, but you're not quite sure (and you don't want to look foolish by asking a daft question) then this book is for you.

If you have been thinking of starting your own business and haven't got it going yet because a fear of finance is stopping you or blocking you, then this book is also for you! It will help remove one of the barriers that may be in the way for you to take the leap forward, improving your understanding of the basic financial aspects of business.

If you have a job and are involved in controlling budgets, or maybe in meetings where the finance language that is used is something that you don't understand. Or perhaps you're too afraid to ask the questions, then this book will be a good kick start to become more confident in basic finance. It will allow you to have a very basic understanding, so that you can start asking the right questions without the fear of being made to look stupid.

"The true measure of success is how many times you bounce back from failure."
Stephen Richards

WHAT'S IN IT FOR YOU?

This book will help you:

- *understand the basics of finance, from the very start;*

- *ask the right questions of your accountant,*

- *make sure you've got the right type of accountant on board*

- *make sure that no one can ever pull the wool over your eyes in terms of how your numbers work,*

- *understand the difference between your profit and your cash and how that can help you make decisions about spending and funding.*

I'm hoping that you'll find each of the sections in this book very easy to digest. Each one is designed to be read and understood in five minutes or less – and mostly less!

"It always seems it's impossible until it is done." Nelson Mandela

WHO AM I?

I've been a qualified accountant for 20 years and have been lucky enough to have gained most of my experience in family owned and entrepreneurially-led businesses.

"I never dreamed about success; I worked for it."
Estee Lauder

Having worked in a lot of different industry sectors and in roles from Managing Director, through Operations and Finance, I can safely say I've seen most of the business outcomes possible, from start-ups through the full spectrum of business ups and downs including liquidations and closures.

In 2002, I set up my very first "proper" business (I've been finding a way of making money since my pre-teen years!), taking it from zero to a turnover of £4.5m in less than three years. Through that period, I was acquiring other businesses from business owners who didn't understand how to extract more value from their businesses. Most didn't have clarity on their numbers, with many barely understanding what their profitability was. It made it very difficult for them to plan growth or even to understand some of the risks that they might have been taking.

Many of these businesses were stuck in low-profit doldrums and couldn't see a way out other than to sell their enterprise for less than they planned or dreamed of.

"It is in your moments of decision that your destiny is made."
Tony Robbins

Since selling my first business (it's still going strong under new management!), I've worked with other entrepreneurs helping them grow, change and sometimes exit their businesses. Along the way showing them how to understand their numbers and the factors that drive the cash – resulting in sustainable growth and often a full or partial (and high value) sale of their businesses.

My successes include:

- *Starting successful new businesses from scratch to nearly £5m turnover in less than 3 years;*

- *Adding £1m to the bottom line of a business services company within 8 months;*

- *Taking a technology business from virtual bankruptcy through to an eight-figure exit and cash in the bank within 18 months;*

- *Transforming a family owned multi-industry company, enabling them to achieve a nine-figure exit when the next generation of that family didn't want to take the business over.*

It's been an interesting and varied journey, and I'd like to share with you some of the knowledge to help you overcome a fear of numbers and start to understand how to use the numbers in your business for better decision making.

So – let's dive in.....

"A book laying idle on a shelf is wasted ammunition. Like money, a book should be kept in constant circulation."
Henry Miller

WHERE TO START?

Throughout this book, I am going to use a lot of visual examples. I have prepared a set of fictitious numbers, based on a company that buys goods, converts them into finished goods and then sells them to locations that require packing and shipping costs.

It's important not to worry about the description of the items; these are completely interchangeable with whatever your business descriptors are.

Any similarity to real life businesses is entirely coincidental!

You will also find space to work on your own numbers so you can apply this new knowledge and understanding directly to your own business numbers.

Notes:

"Financial freedom is a mental, emotional and educational process."
Robert Kiyosaki

TRIAL BALANCE

"Life is like riding a bicycle, to keep your balance you need to keep moving on."
Albert Einstein

To de-myth and de-mystify some of the language in finance, I thought it was worth starting with one very commonly misunderstood term! The **TRIAL BALANCE**…..

One of the most common ways of referring to a company's accounting data is the TRIAL BALANCE (sometimes referred to as an extended trial balance). It is a book-keeping term.

15

The TRIAL BALANCE is a list of the account entries in summary that when all the credits and debits are added together, they add up to zero.

Just for the avoidance of doubt every transaction in business has TWO parts – and equal and opposite debit and credit.

A trial balance is the start of a company's accounts, but it is not a financial statement and is a purely internal check that all the transactions of a company's accounts are recorded correctly. It is called a trial balance because when all the transactions are recorded through double entry book-keeping, the list of debits and credits should always add up to zero!

Notes:

5-Minute Finance

Example Trial Balance for January (showing where the values go in Financial Statements)

Trial Balance	Debit	Credit	
Fixed assets:			
Equipment	7,500		Balance sheet
Vehicles	5,000		Balance sheet
Equipment Depreciation		(63)	Balance sheet
Vehicle Depreciation		(83)	Balance sheet
Stock	5,000		Balance sheet
Debtors	2,000		Balance sheet
Cash	675		Balance sheet
Creditors		(3,500)	Balance sheet
Loans		(6,883)	Balance sheet
Corporation Tax		(7,900)	Balance sheet
Sales		(8,000)	P&L
purchases	2,320		P&L
packing materials	240		P&L
shipping	160		P&L
shipping insurance	80		P&L
Staff wages	2,500		P&L
Office costs	150		P&L
Office rent, rates and utilitie	500		P&L
Insurance	200		P&L
Loan interest	58		P&L
Depreciation	146		P&L
Share Capital		(100)	Balance sheet
Retained profit from prior y		0	Balance sheet
	26,529	(26,529)	0

(total is zero!)

17

The list of entries in the trial balance are split into items recorded in the PROFIT AND LOSS STATEMENT or the BALANCE SHEET which make up the company's financial statements.

- *The **Profit and Loss Account** shows the trading between two dates over a period of time.*

- *The **Balance Sheet** shows the position of the company at a single point in time where assets and liabilities are identified – and allows recognition of the timing difference between when sales or costs happen and when they are paid for.*

Don't worry about the numbers just yet. This trial balance shows that the accounts all add up to zero and where each part of the Trial Balance appears in the Financial Statements.

"The best way to predict the future is to create it."
Peter Drucker

18

FINANCIAL STATEMENTS

"That is a good book which is opened with expectation and closed with profit."
Amos Bronson Alcott

Within a business, all the numbers come together at least once a year when you prepare the year-end accounts which, for most people is an inconvenience resulting from the legal requirement to complete a tax return!

As a business owner, you will typically hand over all the accounting paperwork to an accountant, who you only see once a year. Possibly twice if they are renegotiating their fees! If the business is larger or growing, you may have a book-keeper who is using some cloud accounting software or an accounting system.

It is possible that you literally hand over a bag of receipts to your accountant! Certainly, for many sole traders, this is one of the most common scenarios that I hear about from some of my colleagues who are practice accountants.

So, once you have sent all the business transaction data to your accountant at the year-end, after a few weeks or months, generally, they will send you the **FINANCIAL STATEMENTS** (if your company is Limited) or your **TAX RETURN** (if you are a sole trader) for your previous financial year.

For a limited company, the financial statements are required to be in a defined format specified by the Companies Act (a legal requirement).

The financial statements are the culmination of all the financial information in your business, and they're important because they tell you exactly what profit you made and how much tax you are expected to pay in the next year.

Statutory Accounts are only a historic rear view reflection of your business.

They tell you where you've been and how you've done, but they're not telling you where you're going. Typically, you'll get them between four and six months after your year end, just in time to make the tax payment to HMRC!

Of course, this is far too late for you to use the numbers for effective decision making because you're halfway into the next year.

Without accurate and timely accounts, it's a challenge for you to know exactly what your business financial position is, such as:

- *How to identify which areas of your business are most profitable?*

- *Are there less profitable parts of your business which are losing you money?*

- *And most importantly, are there parts you should be developing to take you to where you want to be?*

You might have a good gut feel for the numbers in your business, but unless you understand the rhythm of your spending, the pattern of your receipts and the relationship between your profit and the flow of cash you will not be able to make informed decisions about the future of your business.

As your business grows understanding the numbers becomes more important as the risks you are exposed to increases.

"When you learn how much you are worth you will stop giving people discounts."
Unknown

The key financial statements are:

- *Profit and Loss Statement,*

- *Balance sheet,*

- *Cash Flow Statement*

They're all important because they tell you different aspects of your business.

Notes:

The Profit and Loss Statement tells you what's happened in your business between two points in time. Typically, over a 12-month period. If you're not getting regular management accounts during the year, your year-end profit and loss will be the only time that you are able to identify truly whether you're making a profit on aspects of your business;

Example Profit and Loss Statement (Jan-Dec)

ABC Company	For Year
PROFIT AND LOSS Statement	
Income	
Product sales	146,200
Warranty sales	5,200
Shipping premium	4,800
Annual service	5,800
	-
	162,000
Cost of Sales	
purchases	46,980
packing materials	4,860
shipping	1,560
shipping premium	1,680
shipping insurance	1,620
	56,700
Gross profit	105,300
Gross margin	65%
Overheads	
Staff wages	59,000
Office costs	1,800
Office rent, rates and utilities	6,000
Insurance	2,400
Loan interest	700
Depreciation	1,750
	71,650
NET PROFIT	33,650
Net margin	21%

The Cash Flow Statement *shows you where your money has come from and where you have spent it, and what cash the operations of your business are generating between two points in time.*

Example: Cash Flow Statement

CASH FLOW STATEMENT	Jan	Feb	Mar	Apr
Operating profit	1,646	2,946	3,396	3,396
Add back:				
Depreciation	146	146	146	146
Interest	58	58	58	58
Income:				
- change in working capital	(1,500)	(1,000)	950	1,650
- cash injections	-			
Expenses:				
- loan repayment	(175)	(175)	(175)	(175)
- capital purchase				
- tax payments	-	-	-	-
Net cash flow	175	1,975	4,375	5,075
Opening Cash	500	675	2,650	7,025
Closing Cash	675	2,650	7,025	12,100

One of the most common misunderstandings is the difference between "cash" and "profit and loss" although often it can be very similar depending on the complexity of your business.

More on this in detail in the chapter on Cash Flow Statements.

"Nothing is a waste of time if you use the experience wisely."
Auguste Rodin

25

The Balance Sheet, which often bamboozles people and there is a whole section on the balance sheet later in this book, is a snapshot of your business value.

Example Balance Sheet at December

BALANCE SHEET	Closing
Fixed assets:	
Equipment (cost)	7,500
Equipment (cumulative depreciation)	(750)
Vehicles (cost)	5,000
Vehicles (cumulative depreciation)	(1,000)
NET BOOK VALUE	10,750
Stock	4,550
Debtors	2,000
Cash	25,050
Creditors	(3,000)
Loans	(5,600)
Corporation Tax	–
	23,000
Net assets	**33,750**
Shareholder capital	
Share capital	100
Profit and Loss	33,650
	33,750

PROFIT & LOSS STATEMENT

"Profit is not something to add on at the end; it's something to plan for in the beginning."

The profit and loss statement, sometimes called P&L, shows where your income or revenue or turnover has come from and what it cost you to deliver those sales - and ultimately what your profit is. There are different elements of your profit and loss – sales, cost of sales, overheads, interest and tax to name but a few.

27

Sales less cost of sales (sometimes called COGS, cost of goods sold) results in **Gross Profit**, which when expressed as a % is called **Gross Margin**.

Thereafter deducting overheads which will usually include staff, premises and marketing costs, results in your **Operating Profit**. When tax and interest are deducted, the result is your **Net Profit**.

The number of different "profits" might be a bit confusing so let's look at the different parts of the P&L in detail.

Example Profit and Loss Statement (extract of part of the year).

ABC Company	Jan	Feb	Mar	Apr
PROFIT AND LOSS Statement				
Income				
Product sales	7,300	9,000	11,700	11,800
Warranty sales	200	300	400	400
Shipping premium	100	200	300	500
Annual service	400	500	600	300
	-	-	-	-
	8,000	10,000	13,000	13,000
Cost of Sales				
purchases	2,320	2,900	3,770	3,770
packing materials	240	300	390	390
shipping	125	130	155	85
shipping premium	35	70	105	175
shipping insurance	80	100	130	130
	2,800	3,500	4,550	4,550
Gross profit	5,200	6,500	8,450	8,450
Gross margin	*65%*	*65%*	*65%*	*65%*
	31%	25%	31%	31%
Overheads				
Staff wages	2,500	2,500	4,000	4,000
Office costs	150	150	150	150
Office rent, rates and utilities	500	500	500	500
Insurance	200	200	200	200
Loan interest	58	58	58	58
Depreciation	146	146	146	146
	3,554	3,554	5,054	5,054
NET PROFIT	**1,646**	**2,946**	**3,396**	**3,396**
Net margin	*21%*	*29%*	*26%*	*26%*

Notice that the Net Margin changes each month. As the sales increased, there was an increase in overheads in March to cope with the demand.

Businesses often experience a steep change in overheads when their business grows. Knowing your numbers allows you to be prepared for this and the impact on your cash flow.

Notes:

"A salesman minus enthusiasm is just another clerk."
Harry F Banks

INCOME/SALES/REVENUE

Revenue is often called income, sales or turnover and many businesses get obsessed with levels of turnover, but it's important to remember the saying:

Turnover is vanity; profit is sanity.

If you can be selling a product for £100, but if it costs you £105 to produce it then you're making a loss on every single item. A push for more sales in this scenario is an accelerated route to ruin. Understanding your margins (gross, operating and net margins – see more on margins later) is critical when you are growing sales volumes for exactly this reason.

We're just going to stick with revenue for the moment.

It's worth a quick note on VAT and timing.

VAT

All your revenue sales or turnover numbers should exclude VAT. I often hear people quoting their turnover including VAT. This gives the illusion of a higher turnover but is a misrepresentation, because you are including funds that are collected on behalf of HMRC. Your revenue should not include VAT or any other added taxes.

Timing for Reporting Revenue

Sales are only recognised when they have been completed – when legal title has been transferred. A promise by a customer to buy something in October cannot be recognised on the day the order was received (in May for example), though a payment in part or full may be received from the customer in advance of the sale being completed.

You may hear this referred to as the accruals principal.

COST OF SALES

The biggest expense is opportunity cost.

Your cost of sales is, at its most simple, the cost of delivering the sale and nothing more. It does not include marketing costs or the costs of acquiring the customer in the first place.

Cost of sales is the cost of either producing or delivering whatever has generated the sales value. This can include:

- *some staff costs, if they are directly related to the production of the product sold or the services delivered.*
- *the direct and attributable cost of components if you're building or manufacturing something.*
- *the cost of delivering a product or service i.e. shipping costs, travel and fuel.*

For example, if you are a training company then the cost of sales will be the trainer for the day, the cost of materials associated with the training and the cost of the travel associated with the training.

Cost of sales is anything that would not have otherwise been incurred cost wise if that particular revenue or sale had not occurred.

What is your Cost of Sales?

"It doesn't cost anything to be nice to people."
Unknown

GROSS MARGIN

Gross Profit is calculated by deducting the cost of the sales, which is the variable costs of producing, or providing services from the revenue, (sometimes known as sales, turnover or income). You'll often see this converted into a percentage and described as Gross Margin.

Gross margin % = <u>Gross Profit x 100</u>

Sales

Take revenue to be £100, deduct £35 cost of sales and the resulting gross profit is going to be £65 and the GM percentage will be 65%.

Your revenue less your cost of sales is gross profit.

EXAMPLE

Sales	£ 100	
Less:		
<u>Cost of Sales</u>	<u>£ 35</u>	
Gross profit (GP)	£ 65	
Gross margin (GM)	**65%**	

35

Usually, you would expect the gross margin to remain constant over a period of time. If your revenue doubles, then the business will have to buy twice as much to sell, and the cost of sales will also double.

Looking at the variability of gross margin will often tell you whether your business is on track or not. Regular accounts will allow trends to be tracked and identify if something is going wrong quicker.

Work out your Gross Margin:

"Many receive advice, only the wise profit from it."
Harper Lee

OVERHEADS

A company's overheads are all those costs that are incurred even if you didn't sell anything this month. This will usually be your office costs, rent, rates, utilities, stationery, the cost of internet and telephones. It will include staff costs including admin and support staff. Overheads are any cost that would have been incurred regardless of the volume of sales activity.

Your marketing costs are part of your overheads too. You should be able to split out elements of your overheads into groups such as premises, staff, marketing, IT and administration costs. Tracking these numbers allows you to see if your costs are increasing and understand why. More importantly, it means you can take corrective actions quickly.

Additionally, by knowing your costs, you can assess the return on your investment in various activities, such as marketing.

Notes:

EXAMPLE

Sales	£ 100	
Less:		
Cost of Sales	£ 35	
Gross profit (GP)	£ 65	
Gross margin (GM)	65%	
Less:		
Overheads	£ 25	
Operating Profit	£ 40	

Notes:

"The best investors look for undervalued companies with low overhead costs, long-term growth potential, solid earnings and low debt."
Mark Hing

BREAK EVEN POINT

It's essential to know exactly what your costs are, along with your Gross Margin. This allows you to see clearly how many sales you need to break even.

The break-even point is the levels of sales the business requires to cover their costs and make zero profit (but more importantly zero loss!). In the example on page 38, the business is selling enough units for revenue to cover costs. If costs increased, more sales would be required.

<u>Overheads</u> = **Gross Margin %**
£ break even

What is your Break Even Point?

EXAMPLE

In the example, again on page 38, the overheads are £25, and the gross margin is 65%, so the number of sales required to break even is £38.

Sales	£ 38
Cost of sales (35%)	£ 13
Gross profit (65%)	£ 25
Overheads	£ 25
Operating profit	£ 0

If your overheads increase, the breakeven point increases. Establishing the breakeven point means a business can plan the levels of production (and sales!) it needs to be profitable.

"Don't leave it to the law of averages to make you break even."
Mike Caro

OPERATING PROFIT

When you deduct overheads and staff costs from your **Gross Margin** you're left with **Operating Profit**. This can be identified as a £ value but also is frequently shown as a % value too.

Operating margin = Operating Profit x 100
Sales

Tracking the Operating margin % trend shows where your business efficiency is – the operating margin increases when your business benefits from economies of scale.

Example Profit and Loss Statement:

ABC Company	
PROFIT AND LOSS Statement	TOTAL
Income	
Sales	160,000
Cost of Sales	
purchases	56,000
Gross profit	104,000
Gross margin	65%
Overheads	71,650
NET PROFIT	32,350
Net margin	20%

Notes:

NET PROFIT

NET PROFIT is often called the **Bottom Line**. This is the calculation of profit that the company has generated **after** all the costs of the business have been deducted, including tax and interest. Expressed as a percentage, it is known as **NET MARGIN**.

In a similar way to the operating margin, you would expect the company to increase its net margin as it grows because it's benefiting from the economies of scale. Fixed costs should grow at a lower rate than revenues.

Notes:

EXAMPLE (Economies of Scale)

Sales	£ 100,000	£200,000
Cost of sales (35%)	£ 35,000	£ 70,000
Gross profit	**£ 65,000**	**£130,000**
GROSS MARGIN	**65%**	**65%**
Overheads	£25,000	£ 40,000
Operating profit	£ 40,000	£ 90,000
Less: interest	£ 10,000	£ 10,000
Less: tax due	£ 6,000	£ 16,000
Net Profit	**£24,000**	**£ 64,000**
Net margin	**24%**	**32%**

"Those who do not manage their money will always work for those who do."
Dave Ramsey

THE DIFFERENCE BETWEEN PROFIT AND CASH

Operating Profit represents the total sales achieved, less the total costs incurred.

One of the principal differences between Profit and Cash is timing - of money paid for the products or services to make sales and money received for the products sold.

You can make profit without generating cash. And you can also generate cash without making profit.

You need to be very clear that you are both making profit and generating cash. A profitable business that does not generate cash and does not have additional funding will still go out of business due to lack of ability to pay its staff and suppliers.

"Money is not the only answer, but it makes a difference."
Barack Obama

45

Sales are recognised when they are earned, not when the cash is received. Costs are recognised when they are incurred, not when the cash is paid.

More details in the chapter on Cash Flow Statements.

Notes:

"Never take your eyes off the cash flow because it's the lifeblood of business."

Sir Richard Branson

BALANCE SHEET

"The two most important things in any company do not appear on its balance sheet – its reputation and its people."
Henry Ford

The balance sheet is a snapshot at a point in time showing the assets and liabilities and the net value of your business. It shows you what value the shareholders' funds are and, therefore, what the value of your business is, in very simple terms.

It's important to understand your balance sheet because it shows you how to recognise the value in your business and what your assets and your liabilities are.

47

Why is it called a balance sheet?

The balance sheet is made up of amounts of money that are owed to the business and amounts of money that are owed by the business (plus a record of the cash that you're currently holding).

Notes:

Example Balance Sheet

BALANCE SHEET	Jan
Fixed assets:	
Equipment (cost)	7,500
Equipment (cumulative depreciation)	(63)
Vehicles (cost)	5,000
Vehicles (cumulative depreciation)	(83)
NET BOOK VALUE	12,354
Stock	5,000
Debtors	2,000
Cash	675
Creditors	(3,500)
Loans	(6,883)
Corporation Tax	(7,900)
	(10,608)
Net assets	**1,746**
Shareholder capital	
Share capital	100
Profit and Loss	1,646
	1,746

Profit from example profit and loss statement

ASSETS

Assets fall into two main categories – current assets and non-current assets, including:

- *Money that is owed to the business from customers who have acquired products and services but not yet paid for them – also called Debtors.*

- *Stock and work in progress*

- *Cash*

- *Assets are owned by the business, either fixed assets like your computers, possibly property and buildings, possibly machinery. Assets would also include an exhibition stand for example. These are fixed assets.*

- *Assets created or purchased by the company that are not physical – this includes patents, intellectual property and goodwill. These are called intangible fixed assets.*

FIXED ASSETS

Fixed assets are non-current assets because they cannot be easily or routinely converted into cash.

Fixed assets are owned by the company, such as computer equipment and machinery that's used to produce products. It will also include the tables and the chairs in the office, and possibly telecoms equipment. Fixed assets will be items that you have purchased for the business that have a long (over one year) economic value to the business.

For example, you buy a piece of machinery that produces your widgets, and you pay £100,000 for this equipment.

The machine works at producing hundreds of thousands of widgets over, let's say, the next five years (often it's much longer!) It would be a misrepresentation of your profits to show a reduction of £100,000 in one year, then have a huge rise in the following year profits because you haven't spent money on equipment. A more accurate reflection of profitability would be to take account of the economic value that is being provided by that piece of equipment across all the years it is in use. This is called Depreciation.

"Accountants are Cowboys of Information."
David Foster Walace

What Fixed Assets does your business have?

DEPRECIATION

Depreciation is the allocation of the economic value that is used in a financial period, of the assets that the business has made use of. Depreciation is applied to both the Profit and Loss Statement as utilisation of the economic value of the asset AND to the Balance Sheet as a reduction of the on-going value of the asset.

Going back to our widget making machine. We know it's going to cost us £100,000 and we know that it's going to produce widgets over five years, or more so we apply the right amount of depreciation to the profit and loss statement, i.e. 20% or one-fifth of the £100,000 is deducted from our profits as a non-cash overhead.

In the example company, a machine was purchased at the cost of £7,500, and it has an economic lifespan of 10 years:

Example

Cost of Acquisition: £7,500

Economic life: 10 years

Depreciation: $\frac{£7,500}{10} =$ £750 p.a.
(£62.50 p.m.)

Now this means there is a distinct difference between cash and profit because our profit wouldn't be hit by the full £7,500 purchase but cash most definitely would.

Cash would not be reduced by depreciation because it's a nominal sum but our profit would. Fixed assets are recorded in the Balance Sheet at their original cost and are slowly diminished in value over the period of their economic viability by the application of depreciation.

Notes:

"Surround yourself with Assets not Liabilities."

Unknown

EXAMPLE (Balance Sheet impact)

BALANCE SHEET	Jan	Feb	Mar	Apr
Fixed assets:				
Equipment (cost)	7,500	7,500	7,500	7,500
Equipment (cumulative depreciation)	(63)	(125)	(188)	(250)
Vehicles (cost)	5,000	5,000	5,000	5,000
Vehicles (cumulative depreciation)	(83)	(167)	(250)	(333)
NET BOOK VALUE	12,354	12,208	12,063	11,917

depreciation

NOTE: Net book value is the amount shown on the balance sheet at every period (in this case every month), and the same value is added to overheads in the P&L. (See page 56.)

Notes:

55

EXAMPLE (Profit and Loss impact)

ABC Company	Jan
PROFIT AND LOSS Statement	
Income	
Product sales	7,300
Warranty sales	200
Shipping premium	100
Annual service	400
	-
	8,000
Cost of Sales	
purchases	2,320
packing materials	240
shipping	125
shipping premium	35
shipping insurance	80
	2,800
Gross profit	5,200
Gross margin	65%
	31%
Overheads	
Staff wages	2,500
Office costs	150
Office rent, rates and utilities	500
Insurance	200
Loan interest	58
Depreciation	146
	3,554
NET PROFIT	**1,646**
Net margin	21%

Notes:

CURRENT ASSETS

Current assets are any assets that can be and will be converted easily into cash and includes stock, work in progress, debtors and cash.

Current Assets

BALANCE SHEET	Closing
Fixed assets:	
Equipment (cost)	7,500
Equipment (cumulative depreciation)	(750)
Vehicles (cost)	5,000
Vehicles (cumulative depreciation)	(1,000)
NET BOOK VALUE	10,750
Stock	4,550
Debtors	2,000
Cash	25,050
Creditors	(3,000)
Loans	(5,600)
Corporation Tax	-
	23,000
Net assets	**33,750**
Shareholder capital	
Share capital	100
Profit and Loss	33,650
	33,750

What is the value of your current assets?

"Honesty and integrity are by far the most important assets of an entrepreneur."
Zig Ziglar

DEBTORS

Debtors are customers who you have sent an invoice to, but the invoice is still due to be paid. Your customer owes you a debt which is why they're called debtors. Sometimes debtors don't or resist paying!

I strongly recommend you have a mechanism for consistently following up invoices and requesting payment to ensure that your customers pay on a timely basis. For some customers' it is common practice to only pay when asked, so it's important to ask for payment at the right time.

You should also have a credit policy to make sure that you don't sell to customers who have no capability of paying. A credit policy is a routine that your business should run to make appropriate credit checks on customers to ensure they have the capacity to pay for the products and services they buy from you. Asking other suppliers for references is part of most credit check processes.

Every now and again a business will experience something called a bad debt. This is where the debtor has no capacity to pay even when you chase them. Once the debt looks unlikely to be collected, you cannot show it as an asset in your balance sheet, and you must write it off.

If you experience difficulties in getting customers to pay you, there are some easily deployable ways to get paid, shown on page 62.

Do you have customers who don't pay on time?

"A small debt produces a debtor; a large debt produces an enemy"
Pubilius Syrus

GETTING PAID

The secret to not experiencing late payment is in the systematic and consistent application of credit control. At its most basic, your system should involve maintaining good relationships with your customers.

Do not be afraid to call your customers up and ask for payment if it is due. Delays in payments may occur due to oversight, so a friendly reminder is OK. Being proactive and letting customers know you are expecting their payments a few days in advance is a good habit to have, and one your customers will quickly get used to.

See an example sequence that follows:

STEP 1 - Reminder: Due date – 5 days
The attached invoice is due for payment in 5 days. If there are any issues that are currently blocking this payment, please let us know. Kindly forward payment to:
Bank Account:
Bank sort code:
Payee:

STEP 2 - 1st Chase: Due date + 7 days
The above invoice was due to be received on dd-mm-yyyy. If there is a reason for non-payment please contact EMAIL ADDRESS. We kindly request you forward payment to:
Bank Account:
Bank sort code:

Payee:

STEP 3 - 2nd Chase: Due date + 14 days
**Liaise with project / sales lead if necessary to find out if there is a reason for non-payment > Action required > Feedback to finance department:
The above invoice is considerably overdue. As we have not been made aware of any reason for non-payment kindly submit your payment to the details below and inform me of an expected payment date:
Bank Account:
Bank sort code:
Payee:

STEP 4 - 3nd Chase: Due date + 28 days
**Liaise with project / sales lead to make sure no relationship management is needed > Email contact:
The above invoice is now significantly overdue. Interest shall be charged at the Bank of England base rate plus **x% (whatever is in your terms and conditions)** as per our terms and conditions. To avoid legal debt recovery action please pay soonest.
Bank Account:
Bank sort code:
Payee:

Write your own debt-chasing sequence:

"To fear what you do not understand is to mistake ignorance for safety."
Ginn Hale

WORKING CAPITAL

Working capital is effectively the oil that keeps the engine of a business working. If you don't have any oil, the engine will seize. If a business cannot meet its obligations when they fall due, the business will cease to be a going concern. A business must continue to be a going concern. Otherwise it is unable to trade and must go into liquidation.

Working capital is the capital being used to run the day to day operations of the business. It is the current assets (debtors, stock) and the current liabilities (creditors and short-term debt) and cash or overdrafts.

> What is the working capital demand in your business?

Stock and Work in Progress (WIP)

A business will buy products from suppliers and, in the case of manufacturing, convert them into products that are sold as finished goods. In the case of retail businesses, the products are purchased from wholesalers and resold. The products form stock which ties up cash in the business while waiting to be sold.

Do you have stock and Work in Progress?

"We make a living by what we get, but we make a life out of what we give."
Winston Churchill

Working Capital Cycle

The time between buying components, converting to finished goods and selling the product is your working capital cycle. If you are selling services the working capital cycle is the time between providing the services and getting paid – usually you will have paid staff wages and expenses as part of the service delivery.

Understanding what you're working capital cycle is will help you understand whether you need funding if you make plans to grow the business.

Notes:

Example (Very Simple)

- *You order some goods from your supplier for delivery 1st May*

- *You have 30 days' credit from the supplier, so you expect to pay for goods 30th May*

- *Conversion to goods for sale takes two weeks (goods ready for sale by 15th May) – so technically you could sell the finished goods BEFORE having to pay the supplier for the component parts!*

- *Average time to sell items (i.e. move finished goods from stock and complete sale) takes four weeks – therefore sale date would be 15th June, with the average customers taking 30 days' credit.*

- *Expected cash from sales 15th July*

Therefore, cash is tied up in your stock for six weeks (from 30th May through to 15th July).

Work out your working capital cycle:

Working Capital Ratios

Stock turnover

This measures the number of days it takes for a business to sell its stock (on average). It is measured using the average stock holding and divide it by the cost of sales, all multiplied by 365 days:

$$\underline{\text{Average stock £}} \quad x \quad 365$$

Cost of Sales £

You can find the average stock by taking the average of the opening and closing stock in your annual accounts.

Work out your stock turnover:

"Every decision you make in business has a financial consequence."
Barbara Vrancik

Debtor turnover

This measures the average number of days it takes to collect money from customers:

Average trade debtors £ **x** **365**

Sales £

You can find the average trade debtors by taking the average of the opening and closing debtors in your annual accounts.

Work out your debtor turnover:

Creditor turnover

This measures the average number of days it takes to pay money to suppliers:

Average trade creditors £ **x**   **365**

Purchases £

You can find the average trade creditors by taking the average of the opening and closing creditors in your annual accounts.

Work out your creditor turnover:

Purchases are not a number that are recorded in your accounts, and can be calculated as follows:

Opening stock (in the balance sheet)

Plus   **Purchases (unknown)**

Less   **Closing stock (in the balance sheet)**

=   **Cost of Sales (in the P&L)**

Therefore,

Purchases = Cost of Sales + Closing Stock - Opening Stock

Work out your purchases:

"Capital isn't scarce, vision is."
Sam Walton

Some useful numbers for understanding your business resilience are liquidity ration and the Acid Test.

Liquidity Ratio

Overtrading is when a business is trading while being unable to meet their current liabilities or current obligations as they fall due. Many business owners do not understand when they are doing so and the business goes bust as they run out of cash.

The liquidity ration can be used to see if the business is at risk of overtrading. This ratio measures the ability of the business to meet its obligations as they fall due.

Current Assets   **= liquidity ratio**

Current Liabilities

A good liquidity ratio depends on the type of business you have but as a benchmark, two or more is good for manufacturing, and one is reasonable for a service-based business.

In the example numbers for ABC Company:

BALANCE SHEET	Opening
Fixed assets:	
Equipment (cost)	7,500
Equipment (cumulative depreciation)	-
Vehicles (cost)	5,000
Vehicles (cumulative depreciation)	-
NET BOOK VALUE	12,500
Stock	4,000
Debtors	1,000
Cash	500
Creditors	(3,000)
Loans	(7,000)
Corporation Tax	(7,900)
	(12,400)
Net assets	**100**
Shareholder capital	
Share capital	100
Profit and Loss	-
	100

Current assets = Stock £4,000, Debtors £1,000 and Cash £500 = £5,500

Current liabilities = Creditors £3,000

Liquidity ratio = £5,500 / £3000 = 1.8333

(NOTE: The loan, in this case, is a long-term loan).

Acid Test

To get a better feel for how the business is doing, in terms of its cash and its liquidity, take the liquidity ratio and remove the stock value.

The reason why stock is deducted is because stock is often not easily converted into cash, it relies entirely on sales activity, and this cannot always be effectively predicted. Having a large amount of stock, and not being able to convert it into cash quickly will impact the company's liquidity and its ability to meet its obligations. This is one of the critical factors in businesses failing.

This gives you a better idea of how capable the company is of meeting its obligations as they fall due and a better view of the immediate liquidity or the ability of a company to satisfy its cash demands.

Current Assets Less Stock = Acid Test

Current Liabilities

In the example numbers for ABC Company:

Current assets = Debtors £1,000 and Cash £500 = £1,500

Current liabilities = Creditors £3,000

Acid test = £1,500 / £3000 = 0.5

Work out your liquidity ratios:

"The biggest mistake a small business can make is to think like a small business."
Unknown

LIABILITIES

Your liabilities are monies owed by the company. These invariably fall into one of three categories:

- *Creditors,*

- *Taxes*

- *Loans*

They are also categorised as Current Liabilities or Long-Term Liabilities.

Current liabilities are anything that can be expected to be paid in cash within the next 12 months, and this includes short term loans. Anything payable within the next 12 months is a current liability.

Long-term liabilities will often be loans over a period of more than 12 months. Sometimes your long-term liabilities do include longer-term tax liabilities.

Long-term generally refers to anything not due to be paid within the next 12 months.

CREDITORS

When a company owes money to its suppliers, these are called creditors, suppliers have given the company CREDIT (i.e. time to pay). It is common for suppliers whom you have built a good relationship with, will give you 30 days' credit (in some cases longer). You have received the goods which will be recorded in the balance sheet as stock and the invoice (which is simply a demand to pay) needs to be recorded somewhere, and it's recorded in Creditors as current liabilities. So, a creditor is someone that we have made a purchase from who is still owed the money and hasn't yet been paid.

Creditors are the opposite of Debtors

Do you know who your creditors are?

TAXES

Taxes are monies that are due to be paid to HMRC for VAT, payroll taxes (PAYE and NIC) and for corporation tax. VAT may be payable quarterly and Corporation Tax is usually not payable for several months after the accounts are prepared, but both are important to be paid on time as HMRC have significant powers to force payment and will add punitive interest as well as fines for late payments.

Knowing what you owe to HMRC and when it is due to be paid should be recorded in your Cash Flow forecast as well as in your Balance Sheet!

Notes:

LOANS

I have seen many business owners resist borrowing money for their businesses. Pre-2008 the banks were literally throwing money at businesses with cheap, easily available credit being touted to just about everyone. While those days are over, there are still plenty of funds available to companies who are growing and investing in their future. It's just a bit more of a challenge to get the funds released!

With my very first business, I was offered (and took) an open line of credit, up to £6m to start with, for acquiring other businesses to allow my company to grow quickly. For someone who had never had anything more than a car loan of a few thousand pounds before, this was a daunting prospect! I quickly got used to it because of the difference it made to the speed with which that business could then grow.

"The price of anything is the amount of LIFE you exchange for it."

Henry David Thoreau

GETTING FUNDING

There has been plenty of press coverage on how the lack of adequate funding is causing problems for small and medium-sized businesses. As many as 60% of all loan applications are turned down – but don't let rejection on first application put you off. There are many more funding sources than the traditional big banks, many of which are small business friendly.

Most business owners take the first rejection of an application for a business loan as absolute and don't make any further applications to anywhere else.

So, if getting access to credit is more difficult in the post-crash era, why borrow money?

One of the benefits of borrowing money is that you can grow the business without using any of your own cash. By not having to wait till you have the level of funding you will need gives you a lot more flexibility and improves the speed in which to grow your business – especially if you are investing in new premises, more equipment or even expanding your workforce.

NOTE: at the time of writing, Funding Circle will fund expansion for new staff.

Repayments of the capital are made from future sales - the cash allows you to get more sales volumes and accelerates the cash you receive, as long as you have the right margins!

Notes:

"Every day is a loan, spend it wisely."
Unknown

The additional benefit is that the interest associated with debt is tax deductible, therefore the interest reduces the taxable profit of the company and less tax is paid. One way of looking at this is it reduces the impact of your interest payments by the tax benefit received.

EXAMPLE (Profit and Loss impact)

	Loans	No loans
Operating profit	£ 85,000	£85,000
Less: interest	£ 10,000	£ 0
Less: tax due	*£ 15,000*	*£17,000*

"The best way to teach your kids about taxes is to eat 30% of their ice cream."
Bill Murray

Notes:

SHAREHOLDERS FUNDS

The Balance Sheet also shows the amount of money that, if the company was to liquidate all the assets and liabilities at the current values, the shareholders could expect to receive.

Shareholder's funds are simply a sum of the assets, less the liabilities. Or if you want to look at it a different way, the shareholder's funds plus the liabilities equals the total assets. And typically, your balance sheet will show the assets, less the liabilities, less the shareholder's funds, and that should come back to zero. This is why it's called the balance sheet.

Shareholder's funds are simply the amount of money that would be returned to the shareholders if the company ceased to exist. In simple terms, if the business was to close today and be liquidated and all the balances converted into cash then this would be the amounts of money that the shareholders would walk away with. It's shown on the balance sheet as a liability because it is the amount of money that the business owes to the shareholders.

NOTE: A word of caution. The Shareholders Funds are NOT the sale value of the company. Additionally, if the company were to close, even voluntarily, it may not recover the full value of its assets in cash.

HOW A COMPANY IS FUNDED

Every company starts off with raising some cash, regardless of the value, either from the founders or by going and raising it from investors. I have started businesses with £100 and a laptop using Costa as my office, equally I have raised nearly £1m of shareholder investment and borrowed heavily from the banks to start another more complicated but instantly profitable company.

When trading as a sole trader, then you and your business are linked and there is no real separation of your business identity and your personal identity.

By contrast, a Limited company is a separate legal entity, (think of it as a separate individual), and it must have at least one shareholder, and at least one director. A Limited Company can enter into contracts, borrow money and get investment from 3rd parties in its own name!

A new company uses the start-up cash to buy the assets that it needs to fund trade and generate profit. This profit is then turned into more cash, although profit is not the same as cash.

When a company is generating cash from its profitable activities, it can either choose to reinvest the cash in more stock or other assets to generate greater profits, or it can return the cash to the shareholders. When a company is growing, it often needs more cash than it's generating.

Two sources of cash can be available to a company:

- **Equity** - *this is the shareholders putting in more of their own additional cash generally for a longer-term commitment;*

  or

- **Borrowings**, *often known as debt, frequently coming from banks or investors who would rather loan the money than commit the money, in terms of shareholding.*

How is your business funded?

Borrowings and Debt

When money is borrowed, there will be interest attached to the repayments. And the interest levels will be a direct reflection of the risk that the lender feels they are taking.

Secured Loans are borrowings supported by a repayment promise from the shareholders, or against assets within the business. With the money secured against something that has a cash value, it's likely to attract a lower level of interest. The lender is mitigating their risks.

Unsecured loans are lent in good faith based on the business performance historically; then it's usual to attract a higher level of interest. The lender is taking a bigger risk and expects to receive a higher rate of interest.

Are your loans secured or unsecured?

What's critical to understand when borrowing money, is:

- *what the repayments will be in terms of cash that goes out of the business;*

- *the timing of the payments; and*

- *how you're going to generate the surplus cash required to make those repayments (more sales, better productivity, bigger margins for example)*

Notes:

"A bank is a place that will lend you money if you can prove you don't need it."
Bob Hope

What is EBITDA?

You may have heard or seen the phrase E-B-I-T-D-A. EBITDA is often used as a base value that can be applied to a business when looking to sell. The EBITDA "multiple" depends on your industry and a number of other factors. It's a very blunt instrument to measure the economic value of your business. It is not, by any means the only method of valuing your business. (There are whole other books written on this subject).

Earnings Before Interest, Tax, Depreciation & Amortisation.

Earnings are your net profit before you've charged the cost of borrowing. Depreciation and amortization are simply the spreading of the economic value of a larger purchase of fixed assets. Depreciation being the spreading of the cost of tangible fixed assets, such as machinery and cars.

Amortisation is the spreading of the economic value of intangible assets, for example, goodwill, intellectual property or patents, for example. There are specific accounting rules for intangible assets which you should discuss with your accountant.

"You only live once, but if you do it right, once is enough."
Mae West

5-Minute Finance

CASH FLOW STATEMENT

"Many small businesses would rather face an angry barbarian horde than tackle their cash flow statement."
Nicole Fende

The Balance Sheet and the Profit and Loss Statement work in relation to each other to show the cash flow statement, which is the movement of cash in your business.

A Cash Flow Statement is NOT always included with the statutory accounts that the Accountant prepares at the end of the financial year. It is an essential part of any management accounts reports you should ask your accountant for.

93

As your business grows, getting clarity on your numbers on a regular basis becomes critical to your decision making. But remember the Cash Flow Statement, like all the other Financial Statements, is backward looking. Putting together a Cash Flow Statement is an essential part of managing your business.

The cash flow statement is:

- *Net Profit,*

- *Adding back any non-cash items that were in the profit and loss such as depreciation;*

- *Taking off any capital expenses that have been incurred such as any purchase of fixed assets and;*

- *Recognising the change in working capital.*

Notes:

In recognising how many debtors have paid us and how many suppliers we have paid and any tax payments that have been made, our closing cash figure which will be shown on the balance sheet as the balance of cash, either as an asset with cash reserves or as a liability if there is an overdraft.

The cash statement shows you what you've spent your cash on and where you've generated your cash from in the past. It can be broken down into a more detailed analysis so that you can clearly identify, for example, profitable parts of the business especially if your business has a diverse offering.

Example (extract of cash flow statement)

CASH FLOW STATEMENT	Jan	Feb	Mar	Apr
Operating profit	1,646	2,946	3,396	3,396
Add back:				
Depreciation	146	146	146	146
Interest	58	58	58	58
Income:				
- change in working capital	(1,500)	(1,000)	950	1,650
- cash injections				
Expenses:				
- loan repayment	(175)	(175)	(175)	(175)
- capital purchase				
- tax payments	-	-	-	-
Net cash flow	175	1,975	4,375	5,075
Opening Cash	500	675	2,650	7,025
Closing Cash	675	2,650	7,025	12,100

**Movement in working capital*

**Changes in working capital is the movement in the outstanding balance of your debtors and creditors.

Example of changes in working capital

	End Jan	End Feb	Movement
Debtor	£2,000	£2,500	£ 500 inc asset
Creditors	(£3,500)	(£2,500)	£1,000 dec liability
Stock	£5,000	£4,500	£ 500 dec asset

Working Capital

	£3,500	£4,500	£1,000 inc assets

Where working capital has increased, there is MORE cash tied up in stock, debtor and creditors – the cash flow statement reflects this by reducing the cash balance by the net effect of the movement.

If the working capital decreases, there is LESS cash tied up in the running of the business. This is a trend worth following as it allows you to spot when the business is increasing its working capital, which can quickly reduce your ability to pay your liabilities on time.

What's your working capital movement?

MANAGEMENT ACCOUNTS

Most business owners have one set of annual statutory accounts that can only be prepared after the financial year-end. These may not even be presented until months after the trading for the previous year has concluded. Savvy business owners, the ones who really understand their numbers, get regular Management Accounts.

Management accounts are not the same (but can be similar) to statutory accounts (which are also called financial accounts).

Financial accounts are designed to make it easy for your accountant to prepare your tax returns.

Management accounts are designed to make it easier for you to make commercial decisions!

Often prepared monthly and in some cases quarterly, Management Accounts show a more immediate picture of exactly how a company is performing.

If you have management accounts every month and I recommend that you have them within 5 to 10 working days, then you will have a quick and transparent view of whether your company is going "off the rails". The answer to valuable questions such as:

- *Are the margins being maintained?*

- *Has the business got enough cash; and*

- *Where is the cash being spent?*

It will also let you identify whether you're growing and where you need to invest your time and effort. If you have a budget/business plan, management accounts allow you to track how the business is performing against that plan

Each business will have its own unique information needs and this is where having a growth focused, commercially savvy accountant on board comes in – you need the right information, at the right time, and in a format, you can understand to allow you to make decisions.

If you are getting financial information in a format you don't understand and can't read, then go back to the person who produced it and ask questions until you do understand. An accountant or finance department (if you are in a role where you are getting financial reports) is there to help management make decisions and manage the business (or business unit/department) for optimal profitability.

Here are some simple reports based on the accounts used in previous examples:

Example – P&L Monthly Management Accounts

ABC Company PROFIT AND LOSS Statement	Current month				Year to Date		
	Budget	Actual	Variation		Budget	Actual	Variation
Income							
Product sales	12,000	11,800	(200)		38,000	39,800	1,800
Warranty sales	500	400	(100)		1,500	1,300	(200)
Shipping premium	500	500	0		1,000	1,100	100
Annual service	250	300	50		1,500	1,800	300
	13,250	13,000	(250)		42,000	44,000	2,000
Cost of Sales							
purchases	4,000	3,770	230		13,000	12,760	240
packing materials	350	390	(40)		1,200	1,320	(120)
shipping	100	85	15		500	495	5
shipping premium	200	175	25		400	385	15
shipping insurance	150	130	20		500	440	60
	4,800	4,550	250		15,600	15,400	200
Gross profit	8,450	8,450	0		26,400	28,600	2,200
Gross margin	64%	65%			63%	65%	
Overheads							
Staff wages	3,900	4,000	(100)		12,500	13,000	(500)
Office costs	175	150	25		650	600	50
Office rent, rates and utilities	500	500	0		2,000	2,000	0
Insurance	180	200	(20)		740	800	(60)
Loan interest	58	58	(0)		233	233	(0)
Depreciation	146	146	0		583	583	(0)
	4,959	5,054	(95)		16,706	17,217	(511)
NET PROFIT	3,491	3,396	(95)		9,694	11,383	1,689
	26%	26%			23%	26%	

This method of presenting the P&L statement allows you to compare where you are with a budget. Budgeting is another area of finance that many people struggle with. In some areas of a business, it is seen as a restriction i.e. setting limits on spending for example. For sales departments, it's more likely to be seen as a target-setting tool. Budgets are a big subject, for a future 5-minute series book.

Back to the example

Receiving the P&L report in more detail (In this example different sales types are shown separately, and the costs are also in detail), means decisions can be made on marketing strategy, sales focus and cost control from an informed stance rather than gut feelings.

For example, we can see that warranty sales account for 3% of the total sales value and, on average, service fees account for 3-5% (4% average over the year). If, in the sales process, warranty and services were promoted more, would there be an increase in take up? Being able to ask the question and try, even for a month or two, to increase sales might result in extra revenue for almost no extra effort!

Where customers were willing to pay a premium for faster shipping the company made more profit on this activity, so this is another "upsell" opportunity.

In costs, there is an average of 36% staff costs to sales ratio across the year, but in some months, this was as low as 25% - one question is was that a month when everyone was working to their limits, and there was no slack at all? And where staff costs were 67% is there an opportunity for some employees to work flexibly or use seasonal staff for the peaks?

On the page 103, there is a month by month sheet showing each month P&L data which allows monthly trends to be seen.

This is the same data as on page 100, but presented in a slightly different format.

The important elements of Management Accounts are that you, and anyone else who reads them, understands them so the format should be set to serve the needs of the audience. If your numbers are presented to you in a way that does not allow you to understand them and make decisions, then they are not useful to you. Equally, you need to take the time to ask questions and find the format that suits your needs.

Notes:

The accountant can advise, but you are the decision maker!
Unknown

Example P&L by month

ABC Company	Jan	Feb	Mar	Apr
PROFIT AND LOSS Statement				
Income				
Product sales	7,300	9,000	11,700	11,800
Warranty sales	200	300	400	400
Shipping premium	100	200	300	500
Annual service	400	500	600	300
	-	-	-	-
	8,000	10,000	13,000	13,000
Cost of Sales				
purchases	2,320	2,900	3,770	3,770
packing materials	240	300	390	390
shipping	125	130	155	85
shipping premium	35	70	105	175
shipping insurance	80	100	130	130
	2,800	3,500	4,550	4,550
Gross profit	5,200	6,500	8,450	8,450
Gross margin	*65%*	*65%*	*65%*	*65%*
	31%	25%	31%	31%
Overheads				
Staff wages	2,500	2,500	4,000	4,000
Office costs	150	150	150	150
Office rent, rates and utilities	500	500	500	500
Insurance	200	200	200	200
Loan interest	58	58	58	58
Depreciation	146	146	146	146
	3,554	3,554	5,054	5,054
NET PROFIT	**1,646**	**2,946**	**3,396**	**3,396**
Net margin	*21%*	*29%*	*26%*	*26%*

103

Example Balance Sheet (month by month)

BALANCE SHEET	Opening	Jan	Feb	Mar
Fixed assets:				
Equipment (cost)	7,500	7,500	7,500	7,500
Equipment (cumulative depreciation)	-	(63)	(125)	(188)
Vehicles (cost)	5,000	5,000	5,000	5,000
Vehicles (cumulative depreciation)	-	(83)	(167)	(250)
NET BOOK VALUE	12,500	12,354	12,208	12,063
Stock	4,000	5,000	4,500	4,750
Debtors	1,000	2,000	2,500	2,800
Cash	500	675	2,650	7,025
Creditors	(3,000)	(3,500)	(2,500)	(4,000)
Loans	(7,000)	(6,883)	(6,767)	(6,650)
Corporation Tax	(7,900)	(7,900)	(7,900)	(7,900)
	(12,400)	(10,608)	(7,517)	(3,975)
Net assets	**100**	**1,746**	**4,692**	**8,088**
Shareholder capital				
Share capital	100	100	100	100
Profit and Loss	-	1,646	4,592	7,988
	100	1,746	4,692	8,088

From the month by month table of Balance Sheet data the trend in debtors, creditors and stock (see the blue line in the chart on page 105) can be tracked.

The orange line is showing the level of sales in the same months as the working capital balances.

Example graph showing levels of working capital and sales

What this shows is that when sales were high, working capital was relatively low meaning, most likely, that suppliers were sending products for conversion to finished goods and those goods were sold before the suppliers needed to be paid.

This is very positive – as long as the stock holding doesn't suddenly build up if sales drop off OR stock holding gets too low to be able to keep up with demand. It's a balancing act!!

105

Example Balance Sheet Movement

BALANCE SHEET	Mar	Apr	Movement
Fixed assets:			
Equipment (cost)	7,500	7,500	0
Equipment (cumulative deprecia	(188)	(250)	(63)
Vehicles (cost)	5,000	5,000	0
Vehicles (cumulative depreciatio	(250)	(333)	(83)
NET BOOK VALUE	**12,063**	**11,917**	**(146)**
Stock	4,750	3,000	(1,750)
Debtors	2,800	1,900	(900)
Cash	7,025	12,100	5,075
Creditors	(4,000)	(3,000)	1,000
Loans	(6,650)	(6,533)	117
Corporation Tax	(7,900)	(7,900)	0
	(3,975)	(433)	3,542
Net assets	**8,088**	**11,483**	**3,396**
Shareholder capital			
Share capital	100	100	0
Profit and Loss	7,988	11,383	3,396
	8,088	**11,483**	**3,396**

This method of looking at your Balance Sheet allows you to put the elements into context. For example, the Net Book Value of Fixed Assets is reducing by the amount of depreciation applied; Current assets (and especially cash) are increasing because of movement in working capital – reduced stock holding, fewer debtors and less creditors.

106

Clarity and transparency makes it easier to understand where you are now and how you got there.

Notes:

Example Cash flow statement (month by month)

CASH FLOW STATEMENT	Jan	Feb	Mar	Apr	May
Operating profit	1,646	2,946	3,396	3,396	1,446
Add back:					
Depreciation	146	146	146	146	146
Interest	58	58	58	58	58
Income:					
- change in working capital	(1,500)	(1,000)	950	1,650	(600)
- cash injections	-				
Expenses:					
- loan repayment	(175)	(175)	(175)	(175)	(175)
- capital purchase					
- tax payments	-	-	-	-	-
Net cash flow	175	1,975	4,375	5,075	875
Opening Cash	500	675	2,650	7,025	12,100
Closing Cash	675	2,650	7,025	12,100	12,975

The cash flow statement in the example business is very simple. There is a single payment of corporation tax in June but otherwise no payments other than the profits generated, movement in working capital and repayments of a loan.

The closing cash figure equals the cash shown in the Balance Sheet and the profit can easily be seen in the P&L.

Your business may not have loans or, indeed may have many different cash outgoings – VAT, staff wages and PAYE, purchases of fixed assets etc. The Cash Flow Statement will always follow the same basic principles as shown here.

Example Cash Flow Movement and Comparison

CASH FLOW STATEMENT	Current month			Year to Date		
	Budget	Actual	Variance	Budget	Actual	Variance
Operating profit	3,491	3,396	(95)	9,694	11,383	1,689
Add back:						
Depreciation	146	146	(0)	583	583	0
Interest	58	58	0	233	233	0
Income:						
- change in working capital	1,500	1,650	150	150	100	(50)
- cash injections	0	0	0	0	0	0
Expenses:						
- loan repayment	(175)	(175)	0	(700)	(700)	0
- capital purchase	0	0	0	0	0	0
- tax payments	0	0	0	0	0	0
Net cash flow	5,020	5,075	55	9,960	11,600	1,640
Opening Cash	7,000	7,025	25	500	500	0
Closing Cash	12,020	12,100	80	10,460	12,100	1,640

Using a similar format to the P&L comparison, this monthly report shows how the company is doing in relation to the budget, or financial plan, for the month and the year to date. This kind of reporting allows you to track if your overall plan is on track as well as the individual months.

In this case, the report shows that for the current month cash was little over what was expected, mainly as a result of changes to working capital – but the year to date is well ahead of expectation, in terms of cash, and this is because of higher profits being generated!

Management accounts and reports are only useful if you understand what they are telling you and you act on it!

5-Minute Finance

CASH FLOW FORECAST

"Happiness is a positive cash flow."
Fred Adler

Having a handle on your cash flow is one of the most important aspects of business management – because cash is the life blood of any business (even not-for-profit and social enterprise).

Money makes the world go round!!

Cash Flow forecasting sounds complicated, but it should be very simple and relatively easy – it's mostly about finding the model that works for your business, that makes sense to you.

111

The more complicated you make something, the less likely you are to maintain it. Equally, if you have someone producing reports for you, make sure you can read them – if you don't understand them, then they are a waste of time!!

Notes:

"The three most dreaded words in the English Language – Negative Cash Flow."
David Tang

Example Cash Flow Forecast Model

Cash Flow Forecast	August	September	October	November	December
CASH IN:					
Cash received from sales	6,324				
Forecast cash in:					
Cash expected from sales	3,000	14,000	14,000	20,000	22,000
Cash from sales of other assets					2,000
Other cash in					
Loans received	5,000				
total Cash in	**14,324**	**14,000**	**14,000**	**20,000**	**24,000**
CASH OUT:					
Regular wages (incl PAYE)	4,000	4,000	4,000	4,000	4,000
Seasonal wages (incl PAYE)	2,000	2,000	2,000	2,000	2,000
Purchases	2,380	4,730	2,730	6,900	8,090
Office rent, rates and utilities	150	150	150	150	150
Insurance	500	500	500	500	500
Loan repayment	175	175	175	175	175
Purchase of new equipment					
- machinery	7,500				
Estimated VAT payments	1,554	2,333	2,333	3,333	4,000
Corporation tax payments	-	-	-	-	-
total Cash out	**14,259**	**9,888**	**7,888**	**13,058**	**14,915**
Net cash movement	**65**	**4,112**	**6,112**	**6,942**	**9,085**
Opening cash (all business accounts)	8,875	8,940	13,052	19,163	26,105
FORECAST CLOSING CASH	**8,940**	**13,052**	**19,163**	**26,105**	**35,190**

This example shows the sample business from August – forecasting the cash position based on the sales being comparable to the previous year. All things being equal, this business should be building some cash reserves and has the capacity for further investment using its own cash.

Each month the cash flow forecast is reviewed and the timing of cash moved according to any changes in circumstances. Always start with the current cash position.

At first using this model might seem a bit fiddly, but with practice, it becomes a useful tool to test the cash resilience of the business.

Using different scenarios, you can see what the cash impact is:

- *on a drop in sales; or*

- *a sudden increase in costs*

- *a large future purchase commitment*

- *a bank loan repayment*

There are endless examples.

If you are considering a large purchase or an expansion of your workforce, using the cash flow forecast will show how your cash reserves will last, and what sales you will need and when. This allows much more effective decision making.

The cash flow forecast is a living model, and changes with every piece of new information added. Understanding what it is showing you and being able to update it and undertake "what if" scenarios is an essential tool in the armoury for knowing your numbers.

Notes:

Don't worry about looking dumb, worry about BEING dumb – ask questions!"
Shannon Denniston

PAYING STAFF

"Excellence is not a skill; it's an attitude."
Ralph Marston

One of the biggest costs that most businesses face is the cost of employees. In larger companies, it's not just the cost of salaries that need to be accounted for, but a wide range of extra benefits often offered such as medical insurance, company vehicles and pensions.

When a small business starts to take on staff for the first time, they are often not aware of the impact of payroll taxes both in terms of the extra costs (Employers National Insurance contributions) and in the timing of payments to staff (net wages) and HMRC (PAYE and NIC).

117

As you can see, there is different vocabulary used for employee costs.

When employing someone, you may have heard those costs called salary and "on-costs".

Notes:

What are "On Costs"?

On-Costs are the additional costs of employment as specified in an individual contract.

Example:

You offer Sarah a job as a Sales Rep, and you are paying her £30,000 plus a car allowance of £400 per month, pension contributions of 3% and workplace medical insurance. The costs of employing Sarah are:

	Annual	**Monthly**
Salary	£ 30,000	£ 2,500
Pension contributions	£ 900	£ 75
Car Allowance	£ 4,800	£ 400
Employers National Insurance	£ 3,800	£ 317
TOTAL	**£ 39,500**	**£ 3,292**

119

NOTE: National Insurance Contribution is 13.8% of taxable earnings over £8,164 (for 2017/18 tax year – this changes every year in April).

Many benefits such as medical insurance are also counted as taxable leading to further taxes as part of the year-end reporting of payroll – see the section on P11D.

Calculate your staff costs:

Payments to HMRC for PAYE

When payroll is calculated, the salary of employees is used as the basis for assessing the amount of tax and National Insurance Contribution the employee pays as well as the amount of National Insurance the employer pays.

Tax (called PAYE – which stands for Pay As You Earn) and NIC (National Insurance Contributions) are deducted from the employee's salary which leaves NET PAY, the amount the employee receives in their bank account.

The PAYE and employee NIC is added to the Employers NIC and paid over to HMRC, generally on the 19th day of the month following the employees pay date. This means that the total cost of employment is made in two payments – one to the employees and one to HMRC. This timing difference is shown in the cash flow statement and also in any cash flow forecast.

Notes:

P11D and Taxable Benefits

When salaries are higher the tax burden increases, and it would be tempting to pay lower salaries and provide valuable benefits to employees as a way of reducing employment tax costs. In my time, I have seen everything from luncheon vouchers, salaries partially paid in Tesco vouchers through to paying for gym memberships and holidays!

Over the years, the government have closed many of the benefit loopholes and made the payment of cash alternatives taxable.

As the value of some benefits could not be added to wages in each month, there is an annual statement of end of year expenses and benefits called P11D. This requires employers to list the benefits provided to their employees – and applies a tax to the total, which then must be reported to HMRC by the 5th July (and paid by 19th July).

"Always treat your employees exactly how you want them to treat your best customers."
Stephen R Covey

Examples of cash equivalent benefits include (but is not limited to):

- *Personal purchases*

- *Medical Insurance*

- *Professional fees, membership dues*

- *Living Accommodation*

- *Cars and car fuel*

- *Vans*

- *Interest-free or low-interest loans*

- *Relocation expenses (generally over a certain value)*

- *Mileage allowances (where paid at a higher rate than the HMRC approved levels).*

In the example earlier of Sarah, the cost of her medical insurance is £3,800 per year plus £331.20 additional National Insurance contribution (as at 2017/18 rates). This needs to be considered when calculating the overall costs of employment.

Calculate your staff costs:

How to get help with HR

While managing staff is outside the scope of this book; I do think it's worth a few words.

A lot of business owners find Human Resource Management (commonly called HR) and managing staff can be quite scary – there is a lot of legislation to keep on top of.

While it can be a minefield, especially when there is a problem, there is plenty of help on hand without having to take on entire HR departments and additional costs.

With the advancement of technology, even small businesses can access an entire HR function at the touch of a few buttons or by picking up a phone.

When you get the right team working in your business, then you can start to see the possibilities and take advantage of opportunities that may have previously seemed daunting. Get it wrong and you can end up in a maze of employee tribunal threats and other red tape.

Every business owner has at least one tale of a bad hire – and usually more than one!

Don't try and deal with HR on your own – get the experts in, they can save you thousands and make sure you get the outcomes your business needs.

Notes:

"You can't teach employees to smile; they have to smile before you hire them."

Arte Nathan

WHAT NEXT?

Hopefully, this book has given you some insight into how easy business numbers can be to understand and what a difference knowing your numbers will make to your decision making.

There are many more complex, and comprehensive books on business finance and other business matters, that with these basic building blocks you may now find more accessible.

If you have a particular challenge, then please contact me and let me know – it might provide the content for the next book!! You can guarantee that if you have a burning question, so do many other people!

5-Minute Finance

If you need more help, then find me at:

 Christine@theprofitfixer.co.uk

 www.theprofitfixer.co.uk

 https://www.linkedin.com/in/cnicholson66/

or call my office on **020 8088 7857**.

WHAT WORDS MEAN....

There is a whole vocabulary in the accounting world that may seem a little strange to you. I've covered quite a lot in the book but just as a reminder (and to add a few other variations you may hear when talking finance), here is a summary of some of the keywords and phrases.

Accounts Payable   Also called Creditors

Accounts Receivable   Also called Debtors

Accrual   A cost that has been incurred but not yet reflected in the accounts. Accruals are liabilities.

Accrued Income

Income that has been earned but not yet reflected in the accounts. Accrued income is an asset.

Acid Test

A liquidity ration ignoring the value of stock.

Amortisation

Matching the "cost" of an intangible asset to its economic life.

Asset

Something that is owned by the company.

Balance Sheet

The position of a company at a point in time, containing assets and liabilities.

Budget

A financial plan for future business operations.

Capital

Investment in a business which includes debt/borrowings and equity (shareholders' investment).

Cash Flow Forecast

A view of possible future cash movements for the business.

Cash Flow Statement

A historic view of the cash position of a company and where the cash has come from and been used.

Cost	An expense to the business
Creditor	Someone/a business who is owed money by the business.
Current Assets	Assets of the company that are expected to convert into cash within 12 months.
Current Liabilities	Amounts expected to be paid by the company within 12 months of the date of the Balance Sheet.
Debt	Investment in the company that typically attracts interest and has an expected (usually specified) repayment date.
Debtor	Someone/a business that owes the company money.
Depreciation	Method of accounting for the matching of the "cost" of fixed assets to their economic life.
Direct Cost	A cost that can be attributed to a product or service that has been sold.
Dividend	Distributed profits to the shareholders of the business.
Earnings	Profits (usually net profits).

EBIT and EBITDA	Earnings (profits) before Interest and Tax – and Depreciation and Amortisation.
Equity	Investment by shareholders that is not expected to be repaid in a specific timeframe.
Fair value	The expected replacement cost of an asset.
Fixed assets	Non-current assets used to run the business.
Fixed costs	Any cost that does not vary directly with the scale and levels of activity. Usually overheads. (Often these will increase in steps rather than in line with volume of sales)
Goodwill	The difference between the fair value of a company's net assets and the price paid by an acquirer.
Income Statement	Another name for Profit and Loss Statement or P&L.
Indirect costs	Any cost not directly attributable to the sales of products or services also called overheads.
Intangible Assets	Non-physical assets such as patents, licenses and goodwill.

Interest	A charge made over amounts of money loaned to a business – usually a % of the amount of a loan that is outstanding.
Inventory	Also called stock.
Liability	The amount owed by the company to another person/company.
Liquidation	Closure of a company and the sales of all its assets to convert everything to cash, creditors are paid, and the outstanding balance is distributed to the shareholders if there is any!
Loan	Also known as debt – amounts borrowed by the company.
Loss	Where total costs have exceeded total income.
Market value	The amount of money an asset can be expected to be sold for.
Net Assets	Total assets less total liabilities - also known as shareholder capital.
Net Current Assets	Current assets less current liabilities – also known as working capital.

Prepayment	An amount paid in advance of receiving goods or services.
Profit	The result of sales less costs, where sales exceed costs.
Profit and Loss Account	Also known as Income Statement or P&L. It shows the trading activity of the business.
Receivership	If a company can no longer satisfy its creditor or other liabilities, it is put into receivership and run for the benefit of the creditors (in contrast to being run for the benefit of its shareholders). Receivership often precedes liquidation.
Refinancing	When a company takes out another loan to pay off an existing loan.
Retained Earnings	Profits that are reinvested in the business instead of distributed as dividends to shareholders (also called Retained Profits).
Sale	Also referred to as Income, Revenue or Turnover.
Share Capital	The value of the shares in a company.

Shareholder	Owner of shares in a company.
Shareholders' Funds	Share capital plus retained profits.
Statutory Accounts	The accounts required by law under the Companies Act.
Variance	The difference between actual numbers and the budget or financial plan.
Work in Progress	Stock that is in the process of being converted from raw materials into finished goods for sale (often call WIP).
Working Capital	The net current assets used by the business to ensure that creditors and other liabilities are paid on time.
Working Capital Requirement	The number of days between when a company pays for goods or services from suppliers and when it receives cash from its debtors (customers).

ABOUT THE AUTHOR

Christine Nicholson is The Profit Fixer, an unusual mix of Chartered Management Accountant with a Law degree and an entrepreneurial spirit. With 25 years' experience working with small and medium-size companies, helping the business owner to change their ideas of success and free them from the tyranny of long hours to working smarter not harder.

She started several of her own successful businesses, and after some time overseas where she found herself accidentally running a zoo; she took a year out to travel before finding new challenges back in the UK.

Returning to the UK in 2010, she was homeless, jobless, single (for the first time in nearly 20 years) and penniless. She had no choice but to pull her life back together and "just get on with it!"

She quickly developed a reputation for moving business owners from ideas to "getting stuff done", resulting in business transformations that have significantly increased both the income and net worth of every business owner she has worked with.

Christine consistently gets her clients increasing their turnover with improved profitability and fewer working hours. Her real passion is working with select business owners who are committed to growing their businesses and becoming truly entrepreneurial (as opposed to working in a job for a company they happen to own). Adding value and creating a business that can withstand the challenges of the future – this is Christine's purpose.

Christine transforms the lives of her clients and is the virtual Finance Director you need to get your business growing profitable now and for the future.

She helps business owners THINK BIG.

She has saved businesses THOUSANDS and helped business owners increase the value of their businesses by MILLIONS.

Christine is NOT a coach – she likes to think she facilitates a business owner learning to really get their business flying!

The real value she adds can be seen in cold hard cash – both from day to day trading and in the exit value of the businesses she works with.

At home, she is the primary carer for a single houseplant and a small vegetable garden. She is also a regular Parkrunner, loves action thrillers and is passionate about life-long learning.

What her clients and colleagues say about her:

"Christine is THE finance director of choice for any company that wants their sh*t nailed to the wall. She is amazing and is recommended by the kind of people that if they said boiling water was cold, I would agree with them… she is that good."

David Goldsmith

Besides Christine's excellent strategic thinking and commercial acumen, I most valued her practical, well thought through ideas and recommendations. Christine gets to good solutions to issues quickly and communicates her ideas clearly and concisely.

Brian Gibson

Working with Christine has been an excellent opportunity to witness her insight and tenacious drive for business transformation. Her eye for detail and ability to challenge the status quo in sometimes difficult circumstances has enabled tough business decisions being made for the right reasons. It was always reassuring to be able to fall back on her depth of knowledge, knowing that any advice would be provided as straight talking, heartfelt, yet diplomatic.

Ian Williams-Wynn

Christine is very capable of parachuting in and seeing what operational and strategic changes need to be made to help a business survive financially. She has amassed years' worth of experience in a number of sectors now and has thus proven her own ability to adapt but also offers clients a wealth of knowledge of different systems and processes, with a view on what works and sometimes more importantly what doesn't.

Jane Howe

"Not just a 'great a book by an accountant' because you're not just an accountant! More of a superhero with a cape."

Mark Hammond

To Mary Louise.

Making our Big
numbers in 2018
and beyond.

Christie
x

5-Minute Finance